MAMMOTH CAVE

By John J. Wagoner and Lewis D. Cutliff

Photography by Chip Clark

John J. Wagoner has been an interpreter in the National Park Service since 1967, when he graduated from Humboldt State College with a degree major in botany and a minor in oral communications. His expertise as an interpreter has been entirely in the area of natural history, beginning at the Blue Ridge Parkway. From the Blue Ridge Parkway his career has taken him to Cumberland Gap National Historical Park, Petrified Forest National Park, Sequoia and Kings Canyon National Park, and finally to Mammoth Cave National Park in 1977. Because of his interpretive experience he is the coordinator for employee interpretive training for the National Park Service's Southeast Region.

Lewis D. Cutliff, a native of Mammoth Cave, began his career as a seasonal interpreter in 1956. He has been a career employee at Mammoth Cave since 1963. He graduated from Western Kentucky University in 1959 with a degree in agriculture and a minor in biology and has done special undergraduate work in administrative procedures from New Mexico Western State College.

We cannot acknowledge all individuals who have contributed; but without the past thirty years of exploration, mapping, study, and research support by the Cave Research Foundation the story of Mammoth Cave would not have been so well known. Their maps, books, articles, and reprints have been invaluable reference sources for the writing of this booklet.

Since childhood Chip Clark has been fascinated by science and the way photography has expanded man's vision of nature. For the past twenty years he has been exploring and photographing around the world, underwater, and underground. Since 1973 he has worked as a scientific photographer for the Smithsonian Institution. His work has been published in *Audubon*, *National Geographic*, *National Wildlife*, *Science 84*, and *Smithsonian* and in books by Abrams, W. H. Freeman Co., the Smithsonian Institution, and Time-Life.

(Cover): Ruins of Karnak
(Inside front cover): Crystal Lake

Mammoth Cave. Published by Interpretive Publications, Inc., P.O. Box 1383, Flagstaff, Arizona 86002-1383.
© 1985 Interpretive Publications, Inc. L.C. No. 84-62868. ISBN 0-936478-08-X.

Produced for Eastern National Park & Monument Association

The story of Mammoth Cave began some 350 million years ago—and it is still being written. Its chapters include the formation of the world's longest subterranean labyrinth; evolution of incredible creatures that have adapted to life in absolute, eternal darkness; prehistoric farmers and miners; more recent miners, entrepreneurs, and promoters; a doctor who conducted an ill-fated medical experiment; scientists uncovering secrets of the mysterious underworld; and intrepid explorers extending known frontiers into uncharted underground regions.

With eager anticipation, visitors descend into the dark, mysterious underworld of Mammoth Cave by way of the Historic Entrance. Legend holds that a hunter named Houchin discovered this entrance while pursuing a wounded bear.

FORMATION OF MAMMOTH CAVE

About 350 million years ago (Mississippian Period) the world was very different than it is today. The North American continent was located much farther south, today's Kentucky area was about 10 degrees south of the equator, and a shallow sea covered most of today's southeastern United States. The warm waters supported a dense population of tiny organisms whose shells were made from the great amounts of calcium carbonate ($CaCO_3$) precipitated from seawater. As these creatures died, their shells accumulated by the billions on the floor of the ancient sea. In addition, calcium carbonate precipitated from the water itself. This buildup of material continued during the 70 million years that the sea covered the Kentucky area until some five hundred feet of limestone (mostly calcium carbonate) was deposited. Late in the deposition of the limestone, several hundred feet of sandstone was deposited over much of the area by a large river system that emptied into the sea from the north.

About 280 million years ago, the sea level started to drop and the continent rose, exposing layers of limestone and sandstone. The stage was set for formation of Mammoth Cave.

During hundreds of millions of years forces at work beneath the earth's crust caused it to slowly rise, buckle, and twist, causing tiny cracks between and across layers of limestone and sandstone. At the same time river systems as we know them today slowly developed. By about 3 million years ago a sandstone-capped plateau stood above the Green River, and a low, almost flat limestone plain extended southeast of what is now Interstate 65.

Weakly acidic rain seeped down through millions of tiny cracks and crevices in the limestone layers. The weak carbonic acid (the same acid in soda pop) dissolved a network of tiny microcaverns along the cracks. As the land continued slowly rising and the Green River and its tributaries eroded their beds deeper, the water table dropped to the same level as the river; and the water in the network of microcaverns drained through the lime-stone under the plateau toward the Green River. The water converged into a few underground channels that became the major drains toward the river, just as rivulets converge into streams aboveground.

As rainwater continued to enter the system, more limestone dissolved, and the microcaverns enlarged; but because the major drains carried the most water, they enlarged the most. Caves were forming.

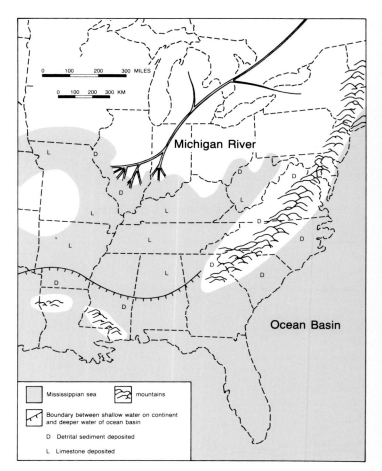

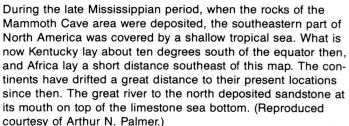

During the late Mississippian period, when the rocks of the Mammoth Cave area were deposited, the southeastern part of North America was covered by a shallow tropical sea. What is now Kentucky lay about ten degrees south of the equator then, and Africa lay a short distance southeast of this map. The continents have drifted a great distance to their present locations since then. The great river to the north deposited sandstone at its mouth on top of the limestone sea bottom. (Reproduced courtesy of Arthur N. Palmer.)

4

Passages enlarge both along vertical cracks across limestone layers and along horizontal cracks between layers. This phenomenon, plus differences in solubility of the layers and fast flow of water created this passage.

As the Green River continued to cut deeper, the water table kept dropping to the same base level as the river. New underground drains were cut at levels lower than the older ones, and the older channels emptied. Thus the oldest cave passages are closest to the surface, and the youngest horizontal passages are the deepest underground—at the level of the water table, where cave passages are still being carved.

CRF photo by Pete Lindsley

FACTORS IN FORMATION OF A CAVE

1. SOLUBLE ROCK — Limestone

a. Shells of sea animals and chemical precipitates fall to bottom of sea.

b. Different layers accumulate and become limestone.

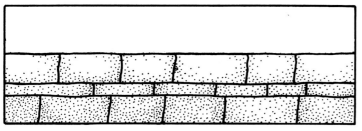
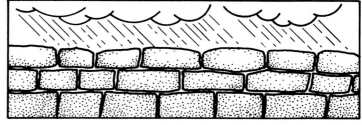

2. LAND, RAIN, AND A PLACE FOR RAINFALL TO ENTER.

a. As seabottom becomes land, earth movements cause cracks.

b. Acidic rain fills cracks and dissolves tiny openings.

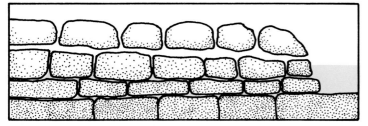
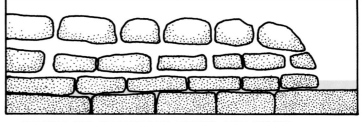

3. A PLACE FOR WATER TO DRAIN.
a. A stream makes a drainage outlet.
b. The cracks that drain most of the water grow bigger. A cave is forming.

4. DRAINS BIG ENOUGH TO ENTER ARE CAVES.
a. As the stream cuts deeper,
b. The upper underground drains are emptied,
c. So we can enter the cave.

Drawing by Mary Phyllis Young, ©Interpretive Publications, Inc., after a sketch by Thomas L. Poulson, CRF

CAVE COUNTRY

As you approach the vicinity of Mammoth Cave, several clues suggest the existence of caves. Road-cuts along highways have vertical exposures of layered greyish rock, often broken into irregular blocks at the top where erosion has widened vertical cracks across the layers. Between the layers you may see the tiny openings in the limestone that are the first stage in the formation of a cave.

The landscape along the highway also has special characteristics. You will not see surface streams or even their branching valleys. Instead, you will see myriads of craterlike depressions called "sinkholes." These sinkholes are places where water slowly filters underground and dissolves the limestone below. Cave drains carry the dissolved limestone away, and the surface soil settles, creating the bowl-shaped depressions. If the tiny sinkhole drains become plugged with soil, then the water cannot drain underground, so a sinkhole pond forms. Occasionally the drain becomes unplugged again, and a sinkhole pond as large as several acres will disappear overnight.

This kind of landscape is called karst topography, and the karst along and to the southeast of I-65 near Mammoth Cave is called the Sinkhole Plain. At its southeast edge, surface streams sink underground, joining the drainage of the thousands of sinkholes. The drains collect tributaries and continue northwest to become the underground rivers of Mammoth Cave.

THE LONGEST KNOWN CAVE IN THE WORLD

Driving northwest from Cave City or Park City, you start to climb a line of bluffs rising some three hundred feet above the Sinkhole Plain. These bluffs are the Chester Escarpment—the border between the unprotected limestone of the Sinkhole Plain and the Mammoth Cave Plateau portion of the Chester Upland.

Beyond the top of the escarpment the plateau is divided into broad, flat, sandstone-capped ridges separated by steep, limestone-floored valleys with many sinkholes. Very little water is able to penetrate the sandstone caprock, so the limestone below is protected from erosion. Most of the early dis-

The headwaters of the underground rivers that formed Mammoth Cave originate in the vast Sinkhole Plain, south of Interstate Highway 65. Thousands of bowl-shaped sinkholes, where water slowly filters into the water system, pock the entire area.

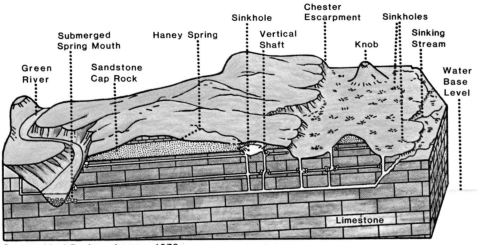

Geographical Review, January 1970

Water in the underground hydrologic system of Mammoth Cave comes from sinking streams, sinkholes on the Sinkhole Plain and in the valleys of the Mammoth Cave Plateau, vertical shafts, and backup water from the Green River. As the Green River has eroded its bed ever deeper, water has drained from the underground river channels, leaving cave passages under the plateau protected from dissolving by the sandstone caprock above them. The oldest passages are closest to the surface, and the youngest are deepest. New caves are still being formed at water base level. (CRF diagram reproduced courtesy of The American Geographical Society.)

coveries in Mammoth Cave were beneath these ridges and valleys, and all the entrances are in the valleys.

A unique combination of circumstances has made Mammoth Cave the longest cave in the world, with more than three hundred miles of mapped passages. First, the karst setting has a large area for potential cave formation. The upstream headwaters of Mammoth Cave are way out under the Sinkhole Plain. Most of the passages big enough for people to enter are under the escarpment, the plateau, and the flat-topped ridges and their intervening valleys that merge into the Green River valley. Springs on the Green River are the downstream outlets of underground rivers such as Echo and Roaring rivers.

Second, the Green River Valley has deepened slowly, but with many interruptions during glacial advances during the ice age (Pleistocene); so Mammoth Cave contains at least three and possibly five levels of major passages.

Third, the limestone is made up of many different layers with different characteristics; therefore, as the underground water sought lower and lower levels, each layer provided a different path of flow. The result is numerous small to moderate-sized interconnecting passages and only a few very large ones.

Fourth, vertical shafts are formed where water flows off the edge of the sandstone caprock and seeps down into the limestone below. These shafts are geologically much younger than the horizontal passages, and they intersect these older passages only by chance. The drains of the shafts, however, eventually join the actively forming passages at the water table, thus adding to the cave's interconnections and complexity.

Finally, the caprock on the plateau protects the older upper level passages from destruction, unlike the situation on the uncapped Sinkhole Plain. There the surface of the land continues to drop, because upper level passages collapse and are eroded away as fast as newer and lower passages are formed at the level of the water table.

Cave passages also collapse in Mammoth Cave as the valleys between the flat-topped ridges deepen and intersect the oldest upper level passages. Usually this collapse results in a "terminal breakdown," but sometimes we can enter the cave at the breakdown of jumbled blocks of limestone and sandstone. The Historic Entrance to the cave is easy to enter because water draining off the sandstone caprock has dissolved much of the breakdown, creating a huge opening to one of the largest passages in the Mammoth Cave system. Because the rapidly flowing water here is not saturated with limestone minerals, it cannot deposit the stalactite and stalagmite formations we think of as decorating caves.

Following pages: At Chief City on the Lantern Tour, part of the ceiling has collapsed. Even though you climb over massive piles of break-down blocks, the ceiling still soars high above your head in this huge chamber.

SLOW AND FAST STREAMS

CLUES TO VELOCITY OF STREAMS THAT FORMED PASSAGES

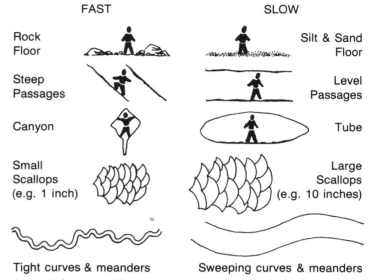

	FAST	SLOW	
Rock Floor			Silt & Sand Floor
Steep Passages			Level Passages
Canyon			Tube
Small Scallops (e.g. 1 inch)			Large Scallops (e.g. 10 inches)
Tight curves & meanders (e.g. 10 feet repeat)			Sweeping curves & meanders (e.g. 100 feet repeat)

Drawing by Mary Phyllis Young, ©Interpretive Publications, Inc., after a sketch by Thomas L. Poulson, CRF

The small scallops in the walls of Sparks Avenue (opposite) and the tight meanders of Fat Man's Misery (above) indicate that these passages were formed by fast streams. Scallops in rock walls show the direction of water flow; the steep side of the scallop is upstream. The long, sweeping curves and oval shape show that a broad, slow river formed Cleaveland Avenue (below).

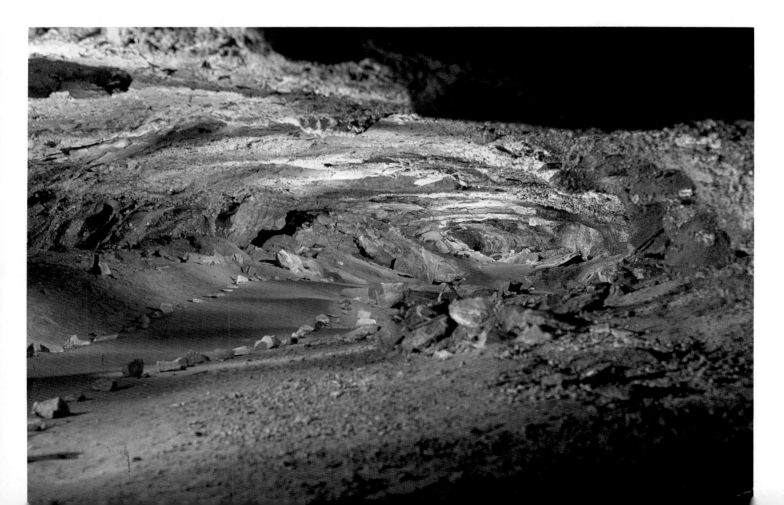

Carbonate speleothems, such as stalactites, are deposited in passages where there is no sandstone caprock above. Water seeps down through tiny cracks in the limestone and deposits calcium carbonate. Thus stalactites tend to form along cracks in the ceiling. When the water drips to the floor, it deposits calcium carbonate there, too, and stalagmites begin to grow upward. If stalagtites and stalagmites eventually meet, they form columns, as in the Drapery Room under Frozen Niagara, opposite.

CRF photo by Ellen Levy

MINERAL DECORATIONS

As water and time enable removal of limestone and the formation of cave passages, so, too, they enable the deposition of "cave decorations" called speleothems. These decorations include both the familiar carbonate stalactites and stalagmites and the unfamiliar gypsum flowers and needles. Although these speleothems seem to grow magically from the walls, ceilings, and floors, they are actually formed by the processes of dissolution and precipitation. The two most common types are composed of the major mineral in limestone rock, calcium carbonate ($CaCo_3$), and by salts of a minor component, sulfates ($-SO_4$).

Carbonate speleothems (such as stalactites) are deposited in passages where there is no sandstone caprock above. Here, vertically seeping water dissolves calcium carbonate and can redeposit it if the water drips into an air-filled passage. The water loses carbon dioxide (CO_2) to the cave air (sort of like losing CO_2 bubbles when you open soda pop). This loss makes the water less acidic, so it is unable to hold as much calcium carbonate in solution. The calcium carbonate is then precipitated as travertine speleothems.

The shape of the speleothems depends on where and how fast water enters a cave passage. Soda straw *stalactites* form on the ceiling by slowly dripping water. As each droplet falls, it leaves behind a minute deposit around its border; and a thin, hollow tube slowly grows toward the floor. If the tube closes and if water drips quickly, a more conical stalactite forms. Fast-dripping water loses still more carbon dioxide as it falls and deposits a

tiny bit of calcium carbonate on the floor, too, to accumulate as a *stalagmite* growing upward. Because the drops splash when they hit, stalagmites tend to be broader than their "partner" stalactites directly above. If a stalactite and a stalagmite eventually meet, the result is a *column*.

Water seeping along cracks on a sloping ceiling deposits *draperies* that are often translucent enough to show banding of colors due to traces of different minerals. Iron, the most common mineral, tints speleothems hues of brown and orange. If water is sufficient, it spreads into thin sheets on the walls and over ledges and deposits *flowstone*.

If there is still carbonate in solution when water reaches a gently sloping floor, then *rimstone dams* and *rimstone pools* may form. The dams start as a deposition on slight irregularities in the floor. A pool forms behind the dam, which continues to grow along the pool's rim. Sometimes whole series of rimstone dams and pools form.

Helictites form when water seeps very slowly to the ceiling in passages below the edge of the sandstone caprock. These twisted, spaghetti-like speleothems can grow in any direction. Part of the explanation is that there is rarely enough water to get to the tip and drip off.

At Mammoth Cave you most often see passages decorated with calcium carbonate near entrances in the valleys where the caprock is gone. In these damp passages (95 to 100 percent relative humidity) the very soluble sulfate minerals are not deposited, because they stay in solution as water moves deeper into the limestone.

Sulfate speleothems (like gypsum flowers) are

14

deposited in dry passages beneath the sandstone caprock. Calcium sulfate (gypsum) is much more soluble than calcium carbonate is and can be carried toward cave passages by the slight amount of water that seeps through the sandstone caprock. The water in the damp limestone is slowly drawn by capillary action into dry passages (85 to 95 percent relative humidity) from all directions. As the water evaporates, gypsum is deposited. At its most spectacular, this mineral ($CaSO_4$) forms white to gold flowerlike structures that seem to ooze and curl from the wall, ceiling, or floor much like icing from a cake decorator's nozzle. In fact, gypsum speleothems *do* grow from the base. This phenomenon helps explain why they can form loose crusts

or blisters and how gypsum growing in limestone cracks can force off bits of limestone and covering gypsum from the ceiling and wall. This process is extremely slow, however, and rotten-looking walls are usually held together by the shining crystals of gypsum in all the cracks and crevices.

Sodium sulfate (mirabilite) and magnesium sulfate (epsomite) also occur in Mammoth Cave, but these other sulfate salts are not deposited unless the humidity is low for caves (75 to 85 percent). Mirabilite and epsomite are much more soluble than gypsum. All the sulfates are important to the story of prehistoric Indians in Mammoth Cave, but other life in the cave predated the Indians by millions of years.

KINDS OF CAVE DECORATIONS AT MAMMOTH CAVE

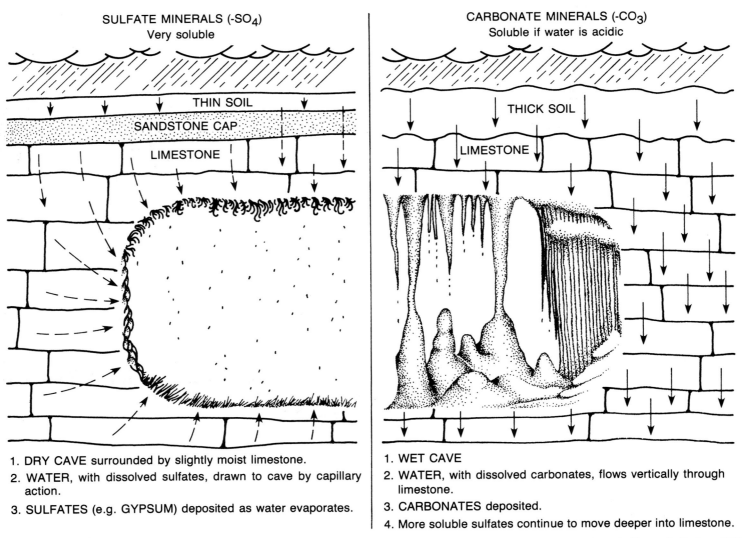

SULFATE MINERALS (-SO_4)
Very soluble

CARBONATE MINERALS (-CO_3)
Soluble if water is acidic

THIN SOIL
SANDSTONE CAP
LIMESTONE

THICK SOIL
LIMESTONE

1. DRY CAVE surrounded by slightly moist limestone.
2. WATER, with dissolved sulfates, drawn to cave by capillary action.
3. SULFATES (e.g. GYPSUM) deposited as water evaporates.

1. WET CAVE
2. WATER, with dissolved carbonates, flows vertically through limestone.
3. CARBONATES deposited.
4. More soluble sulfates continue to move deeper into limestone.

Drawing by Mary Phyllis Young, ©Interpretive Publications, Inc., after a sketch by Thomas L. Poulson, CRF

Grotesque configurations of helictites are deposited by very slowly moving water in passages under the edge of the sandstone caprock.

Beautiful gypsum flowers "blossom" in dry passages beneath the sandstone caprock. The very little water that gets past the caprock into the limestone below is drawn to dry passages by capillary action, where the water evaporates and deposits these minerals.

CRF photo by Pete Lindsley

Rainbow Dome rises spectacularly above the underground trail in the Frozen Niagara area. Although algae and mosses that could provide food for some cave animals can grow near electric lights such as here, most animals avoid lighted areas. All animals ultimately depend on plants at the beginning of food chains, but plants cannot grow without light. Thus, finding food is a big problem in the absolute darkness of caves, but cave animals have evolved unusual solutions to this problem.

PLANTS AND ANIMALS

About 150 species of animals have been found in Mammoth Cave, but only 30 of them have large enough populations to be commonly seen. You will be lucky to see even one or two of these animals on most public trails, although crickets are often seen on the Frozen Niagara and Great Onyx tours. This number is not many compared with the two thousand or so species of animals in local forests and waters outside the cave. Why are there so few species in the cave? After all, the cave does have a pleasant climate. The temperature remains near 54°F (12°C) year around, and the humidity is usually between 85 and 95 percent. Many visitors, in addition to humans, find the cave a comfortable refuge from cold winter and hot summer temperatures.

The real problem in caves is lack of light. Green plants cannot grow without light, and almost all animals—including cave animals—ultimately depend on plants at the beginning of food chains. Some green algae and mosses grow around electric lights on cave trails, but most cave animals avoid these areas. The cave animals depend mostly on decomposed plant material carried into the cave by water or in feces of animal visitors that feed on plant material outside the cave. Both sources of food are scarce in the cave, so few species live there.

Some "cave" animals avoid the food problem by feeding outside. They spend only a portion of their lives in the cave. They are called trogloxenes. This Greek word literally translates to "cave" (troglo) "guest" (-xene). All trogloxenes depend less on sight than we do, so they can find their way in and out of caves in the dark. Raccoons, for example, spend only brief periods in caves during cold periods in winter or hot spells in summer. They have well developed senses of hearing, smell, and touch; but bats are even better at getting around, because they use echolocation. As they fly in the dark, they emit high-pitched cries that bounce back to tell them the location of obstacles or prey.

Bats, such as the grey, indiana or social, and the little brown, are trogloxenes that hibernate in caves. They once used Little Bat Avenue, on the Historic Tour, before the steel plates on the cave gate stopped cold air flow into the cave in winter. The bats needed this cold air to slow metabolism enough for their fat to last through the winter. Increasing numbers of visitors were also a problem for hibernating bats. Visitor activity disturbed bats so frequently that their winter fat reserves were used up before their insect food became available again in spring, so they died. Now the National Park Service protects hibernating bats in Dixon and Colossal caves by prohibiting visits during the hibernation season.

Pack rats and cave crickets are trogloxenes that spend part of every day in caves and reproduce there. Both use chemical trails and touch to find their way out to feed and back to their daytime resting spots near entrances. Near each pack rat's nest is a toilet area, and under each communal cricket roost are black coatings of feces. The feces of both are an important source of "imported" food for communities of cave animals that spend their entire lives in the cave.

Permanent cave animals are of two types. Troglophiles are literally "cave lovers," and troglobites are "cave dwellers." Troglophiles *can* live *either* inside *or* outside caves, but troglobites *must* live in caves.

Troglophiles can live in dark, cool, cavelike conditions outside, such as under litter or logs on the forest floor or under rocks and undercut banks of swift streams; or they can complete their life cycles inside caves. During the dry and warm periods between glacial advances—the most recent about ten thousand years ago—troglophiles that preferred surface habitats became rare, and only those individuals living inside caves survived.

During thousands of generations, troglophiles isolated in caves evolved to become specialized in ways that maximized their ability to detect scarce food and minimized their expenditure of energy. During the same time they lost functional eyes, coloration, and the ability to cope with variable

temperature and moisture conditions. In the near-constant conditions and absolute darkness of the cave, these losses are not a problem; but they do mean that troglobites are evolutionarily "stuck" in caves. Outside, lack of sight and protective coloring would make them easy prey for predators, or they would die as temperatures go below about 41°F (5°C) or above about 77°F (25°C).

What kinds of animals are troglophiles and troglobites at Mammoth Cave? Terrestrial types include familiar beetles, spiders, and millipedes as well as unfamiliar mites, springtails, and bristletails. Aquatic types include fish, crayfish, and shrimp as well as isopods, amphipods, and flatworms.

Troglobitic fish and crayfish are easily recognized because they are so obviously different, with their white appearance and lack of visible eyes. Not so obvious are the adaptations that allow troglobites to find scarce mates and food and to use the little food they do find very efficiently by conserving energy. Careful side-by-side examination of a troglobite and troglophile reveals that the troglobite has larger or longer sensory structures. Troglobitic crayfish, for example, have longer antennae that can be used as feelers and that also have sense organs to detect odors and water movement of prey or a potential predator like a cave-fish. Troglobitic fish have larger heads covered with rows of sense organs that look like stitches. These organs detect water movements of moving prey and

changes in flow of water around their head as they approach an obstacle. Both troglobitic fish and crayfish have slimmer and smaller bodies, so do not need as much food as their stouter and larger troglophilic relatives. The slow, deliberate movements of the troglobites suggest a low metabolic rate; and actual measurements confirm that the rates are reduced as much as fivefold to tenfold. This adaptation allows them to exist with the small and occasional meals that are the rule in the cave.

Seasonal floods influence the renewal of food in caves, so reproductive cycles of aquatic cave creatures are seasonal. They breed when there is enough rain or snowmelt to carry organic matter into caves. This tends to happen in spring, but it can happen anytime from December through June. Such unpredictability is not a problem for small species, like amphipods and isopods, which can reproduce quickly. It *is* a problem for larger species, like fish and crayfish, that need much more food to develop eggs and much longer for their young to become self-sufficient. In many years food is insufficient for successful reproduction. With such problems it is important that animals be ready to try every year at the best time, whenever that occurs. Without change of day length as a cue to time of year, crayfish and fish have evolved annual clocks that enable them to be poised with mature eggs and ready to mate and lay eggs whenever subtle changes in chemistry

A boat ride on the underground Echo River is one of the highlights of a trip to Mammoth Cave. Several specialized species of fish, crayfish, and shrimp live in the cave's underground waters.

Fish and crayfish that live permanently in the cave's darkness lack visible coloring and eyes. What looks like "stitches" on the fish's head are actually sense organs that enable it to locate prey and obstacles. The crayfish's long antennae serve the same purpose.

of the water signals inflooding of organic matter. If they started to develop eggs at the signal, then they would not have enough time to carry their few, large eggs the six months needed for development and hatching. In addition there would not be time for the newly hatched young to grow enough to be able to survive until the next renewal of food.

Cave fish, crayfish, and shrimp spread their high risk of reproductive failure by living a long time. With many attempts they produce just enough young to replace themselves. As with humans, long life makes them vulnerable to toxins, including both heavy metals like lead and pesticides like the relatives of DDT still being used. They and we have no way of completely detoxifying these pollutants, so the toxins accumulate in their bodies with time. In addition, they and we concentrate toxins by eating other contaminated organisms.

Few or no pollutants are produced in the park, but much of the water in the big stream passages comes from outside the park. If there were even a temporary problem with wastewater treatment plants, then incompletely treated domestic and industrial sewerage could get into the Green River, backflood into springs, and enter downstream parts of Mammoth Cave. As shown by dye tracing experiments, a more likely source of pollution in Mammoth Cave is upstream from the Sinkhole Plain. Both point source pollution (such as from a wrecked chemical tanker on the interstate highway or leaking

age from a gas station) and diffuse source pollution (such as fertilizer and pesticide running off cropland into sinkholes) will enter the groundwater and travel to Mammoth Cave. The old saying "out of sight, out of mind" is dangerous in cave country.

SEASONAL CHANGES
Many people find winter the best time to visit the park. There are no crowds of visitors and no annoying insects, ticks, or chiggers. Naked tree limbs form a dark tracery against a cobalt blue sky. Snow often covers the ground, and its ice crystals skitter across the ground in ever-changing waves as the wind blows across the open flats of the ridge tops. The valleys are protected from wind, however, so a walk to a cave entrance can be a delightful experience.

Without foliage to obscure the view, the karst landscape is obvious as you walk off the ridge top and descend past outcrops of the sandstone caprock into the sinkhole-filled valley. With protection from wind, animal tracks remain for days. You will likely see tracks of deer, cottontail rabbit, and squirrel, because these animals eat nuts or browse on buds, twigs, and bark all winter long. You may see both fox and weasel tracks in areas where mice tunnel beneath the snow. You will hear, even from long distances, the raucous "caws" of crows and the harsh slurring "jeeah" of bluejays. Closer at hand you may hear a medley of nasal "yanks" of nuthatch, clear whistled "peter-peter-peters" of titmice, and unmistakeable "chick-a-dee-dee-dees" of chickadees. These birds co-occur in mixed flocks in winter, taking advantage of each other's hunting techniques to find local concentrations of food.

A cold wind blows into the cave entrances, and one often sees ice stalactites and stalagmites there. Among smaller animals, the first life you encounter are hibernating mosquitoes, moths, and daddy-longlegs. The kinds of hibernating bat found indicate the changes in microclimate as you proceed inward. Ceiling carpets of social bats, about 150 per square foot, are in the coldest and windiest spots near the entrance. Looser clusters of little brown bats occur where the microclimate is less severe. And when you see droplets of water condensed on the fur of a solitary pipistrelle bat, you know that you have reached the near constant temperature and 100 percent humidity of the deep cave. Only here will you start to see the troglobites, like beetles and millpedes, that avoid the cold, variable winter entrance zone.

Still farther in, the dry, lifeless passages far under the caprock display special winter holiday decorations of sulfate minerals. With the world above frozen, even less water than usual penetrates the sandstone above, so the passage walls are at their driest. This condition favors the growth of highly soluble mirabilite and epsomite, which may cover all surfaces. Rocks and even dirt trails grow fuzzy with crystals, needles, and hair in especially dry years. Meanwhile, the carbonate stalactites near the entrance may completely dry, thus stopping growth until spring.

As spring approaches, rimstone pools slowly fill again as the soils outside become resaturated with water. On pool surfaces white flatworms glide, using the surface tension; and on the bottoms tiny white amphipods scuttle along. The cave crickets somehow know when the evenings are above freezing as they head for the entrance to forage outside during a late winter thaw. Sometimes they must run a gauntlet of hungry black-spotted orange salamanders whose appetites are also aroused by hints of spring. Surprisingly, the crickets exiting the cave are mostly medium sized. The large ones have matured and are heading deeper into the

cave. They go down vertical shafts to sandy passages where they mate and lay eggs. This does not save them from predation, however, because a quarter-inch "sand" beetle switches its searching behavior to key on sand and starts to hunt for the crickets' eggs. The beetles eat as many as 95 percent of the eggs; but the crickets tend to lay so many that enough escape predation to hatch, return to the entrance to feed, grow, mature, and complete their life cycle.

Spring moves slowly in the cave, but on the surface it arrives quickly as days lengthen and temperatures rise. Spring brings renewal to the surface. The long winter sleep has passed, and the forest awakens. The first warm rains stimulate the high piping whistles of spring peeper frogs in temporary ponds. Their song escalates to a continuous chorus that sounds like sleigh bells at a distance. Serviceberry is the first tree to bloom, showing splashes of white here and there through the bare trees. The pace accelerates as the pastel magenta of redbud blossoms paints the scene. Large white blossoms of dogwood glow like lights throughout the forest. At the end of April the wildflower display reaches its peak. All are seemingly in a rush to flower and set seed before the trees leaf out and shade the forest floor for the summer. The forest is literally carpeted with colors. As many as ten species may bloom in a square yard.

As trees and shrub leaves begin to break from

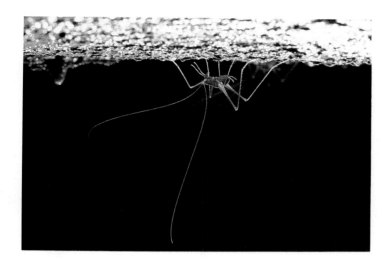

Astonishment gives way to curiosity at a first glimpse of cave crickets, which are often seen on the Frozen Niagara and Great Onyx tours. Cave crickets feed outside the cave and roost inside. Their eggs and droppings provide food for permanent residents of the cave.

their buds, the forest turns a dozen tints of soft green. Insects hatch and start feeding, and migrating birds find a bonanza of inchworm caterpillars in the treetops. Soon thereafter the resident male birds proclaim their territories to prospective mates. The flutelike "ee-o-lay" of the wood thrush and the song of the scarlet tanager, sounding like a robin with a sore throat, are especially distinctive in the forested valleys around cave entrances.

As dusk falls, bats can be seen fluttering slowly and occasionally diving abruptly to capture mosquitoes or moths that have left their hibernating site in cave entrances. A mother pack rat scurries back into the cave to nurse her newborn young in a cozy nest of grass and cedar bark. Among the rat's early spring foods are cave crickets, which are vulnerable because they feed outside almost every night now. During the day a phoebe hawks for prey among a mating swarm of midges. She feeds them to her young in a mud nest camouflaged by bits of moss and lichens. The nest is plastered to a limestone ledge just inside the cave entrance's twilight zone.

Summer can be hot and humid, and both people and animals seek comfort at cave entrances. A cool breeze issues from within the cave, rustling the tree leaves. Just inside, the temperature is the same as it is far into the cave. In the twilight zone, light grows dimmer with distance from the entrance. Along this light gradient vegetation changes

from large and complex to small and simple. Trees and bushes give way to ferns and mosses, then to one-celled algae and molds. Then there is absolute blackness.

At cave entrances with little traffic from people animals can be seen or their signs noted. If you do not see their white tail flags as deer run away, you can see the crushed areas where they have rested on the cool leaves and ferns. The pack rats are not often seen, but you will appreciate their name if you leave belongings unattended. Anything small and shiny, such as car keys, will be packed off to their nest. They eat anything edible, chew up anything that can be used as nest material, and scent mark with urine anything too big to move, just to let you know that you are intruding in *their* territory.

Animals in caves do not make audible sounds, but summer evenings outside are punctuated by a variety of spectacular noise makers. The vigorous oft-repeated "whip-poor-weels" of the whippoorwill can be heard everywhere. Sounds like a barking dog are really a barred owl far away. Close up, this "eight-hooter" sounds like "hoo-hoo, hoo-hoo. . . hoohoo-hoohooaw." It is not hard to imitate, and you can fool the owl into an escalating dialogue.

In fall all life prepares for winter. Its approach is cued by drying in caves and by decreasing day length and temperatures outside. By September many stalactites have stopped dripping, and rimstone pools are drying. Amphipods and flatworms burrow into the bottom, where they will wait for early winter rains to resaturate the forest soil and allow water to percolate into the cave again. Large animals are frantically eating to put on fat. The bats need fat to sustain them during hibernation, and birds need it for energy for long migrations to warmer climes. Pack rats have put on fat, stored food, and reinsulated their nests. They know tough times are near when lack of air flow—with equal surface and cave temperatures—signals the switch from outflowing air in summer to inflow of cold air in winter.

We can see when summer is giving way to winter as brilliant fall colors appear. The green chlorophyll of leaves is broken down and reabsorbed, unmasking the bright colors of accessory pigments.

Frozen Niagara cascades over ledges in a magnificent display of drapery and flowstone formations.

Bats no longer frequent the public areas of Mammoth Cave, because the presence of people disturbs them. In winter thousands of social bats hibernate in dense patches in the coldest and windiest spots near cave entrances not open to the public. The bats need this cold air to slow their metabolism enough for their fat to last through the winter.

CRF photo by Charles E. Mohr

In successional old fields the reds of sumac, oranges of sassafras, and purples of dogwood contrast with the browns of oaks and evergreen of cedars. In climax forests only the canopy colors up, because it is most exposed to warm, sunny days and frost-nipped nights. Below, orange and yellow tinted light streams down through the canopy. As fall proceeds, multicolored leaves rain down, and the forest floor becomes a patchwork of colors. Some tree leaves are all the same color, as with the dull browns of white oak, the bright yellow of tulip poplar, and the brilliant red of black gum. Others are variegated, as with the yellows and browns of hickories, the oranges and purples of ash, the oranges and yellows of sugar maple, and the spectacular bright reds, oranges, and yellows of red maple. This is truly nature's last fling before winter comes again.

THE FUTURE OF MAMMOTH CAVE
As long as we are careful about pollution, even the cave communities dependent on water from the Sinkhole Plain will remain. Meanwhile, the forests of the park will complete their successional recovery. Earlier, the land in the park was used to grow crops, mainly corn and tobacco, in areas flat enough to plow. The steeper areas were used to pasture cattle and pigs and were selectively logged, especially for white oak.

As you enter the park, you will notice a dense successional forest. Yet, as recently as 1941, when the park opened, farms were common; their outbuildings, fields, fencerows, and pastures dotted the landscape. When farming stopped, a young, second growth forest began to reclaim the land. This regeneration will continue through stages of natural succession until the forest becomes a mature climax, some hundreds of years from now. Today only old piled rock "fences" and, in spring, flowering daffodils betray the locations of the former homesteads. More widespread are red cedars still hanging on among taller and later successional oaks. The cedars show where the land was once farmed or heavily grazed.

Successional recovery is occurring fastest on the fertile floodplains of the Green River and slowest on the poor soils on top of the sandstone caprock. Every flood reinforces the zonation of plants tolerant of root submersion and able to take advantage of the nutrients left by deposition of silt. The levee and adjacent "bottom" are typically dominated by silver maple and huge sycamore, the largest a hundred feet high and six feet in diameter. In summer the ground beneath these fast-growing trees is hidden by a solid stand of yellow-flowered wingstem. At a slightly higher elevation grows blue-flowered mist flower or ageratum. The major trees here are red maple and box elder. The favorable growth conditions on these floodplain soils are evident by comparing growth rates for tulip poplar

Water condenses on a hibernating solitary pipistrelle bat far enough from an entrance that the humidity is nearly 100 percent.

here to those on soils of the sandstone caprock. On the floodplain trees add almost an inch per year in diameter, whereas on the poor plateau soils they add only a fifth of an inch per year.

The uplands and valley bottoms quickly lost their shallow topsoils with yearly plowing, so it is not surprising that they are recovering slowly. Severely eroded rocky soils, especially on steep slopes, may remain sparsely treed "savannahs" or "cedar glades" for hundreds of years. In open spaces among trees grow prairie grasses, like little bluestem and Indian grass, as well as prairie wild-

flowers, like rattlesnake master and blazing star. All these plants can grow on the drought-susceptible, thin, rocky soils that remain after intensive farming and grazing.

The most recently abandoned land can be seen along the trail to Cedar Sink and in the Great Onyx group camping area. Shrubs, such as sumac, and trees, such as cedar and oak, are invading from the forest edge; but grasses and wildflowers are still plentiful. These "edge" habitats are excellent for wildlife because they provide both the shelter of the forest and the food of the semi-open areas.

27

Enticing trails lead hikers through second growth forest where nature is reclaiming old fields and pastures where farms once existed before the national park was established.

The winter browse line on the cedars shows that deer have especially dense populations in some years. The deer population of the park fluctuates dramatically from year to year. It increases quickly, with regular twinning and even triplets, after mild winters; but it can crash even more quickly with a combination of epidemic disease and severe winters. In presettlement times big predators, like cougar, probably kept the herds more stable and certainly more healthy. Unlike human hunters, cougars and wolves caught and ate the old, weak, sick, and malnourished along with many fawns. Natural predators are long gone, however, and cannot realistically be reintroduced, so we will have to wait for climax forest to return to see less dense and more stable deer populations in the park.

If you camp, then the ubiquitous, curious, and ever-hungry raccoons will find you. Your chances of encountering other large mammals are increased by traveling long distances at a slow rate by boat on the river or by car, especially along the side roads and the motor nature trail. At dusk and at night animals even come onto the grassy areas along the main roads. Deer are especially common. You often see the eye shine before you see a loping raccoon or a shuffling opossum. The stench of the skunk may be encountered night or day. During the day groundhogs are commonly seen along the roads, and you may be lucky and see a fox. Along the river deer stare out from the woods, and kingfishers perch on branches and dive suddenly in pursuit of small fish. On calm reaches of river, wood ducks float quietly. Muskrat, and occasional beaver, glide across the still surface.

The climax stage of succession does not have high densities of any one species, but it does support the highest diversity of animals and plants. Multiple tree blowdowns provide openings in the canopy that admit full sunlight to the forest floor, thus encouraging vigorous plant growth that attracts many of the early successional animals. But the forest also harbors many species found only at the climax stage. Remnants of never-logged forest show us what much of the park will look like in several hundred years. Of two such areas easily accessible from roads, the Big Woods differs in appearance from upland to valley. On the flat upland the soil is thin and susceptible to drought. Here the only large trees are scattered white oak, black

oak, and tulip poplar. Smaller individuals of these species, along with red maple and flowering dogwood, form a mixed subcanopy layer. The slopes keep these species and add black gum and sourwood. The soil is deeper here, so more large canopy trees grow. The valleys have still more large trees and a more open understory. New species added are beech, red oak, and sugar maple. This combination makes the forest a mixed species climax like that visible along the trail by Mammoth Dome Sink near park headquarters.

This mixed species woods can be recognized as climax not so much by size of the largest trees as by presence of all sizes of each species. Juvenile, adult, dying, dead, and decomposing individuals are present, unlike a regenerating forest with only middle-aged, vigorously growing trees. At climax the dying and dead trees are being decomposed by fungi, bark-and-wood-boring beetles, carpenter ants, and termites—all of which provide food for many animals. One of the most striking of these animals is the large pileated woodpecker. Its black and white plumage with a red "topknot" is the model for Woody Woodpecker of cartoon fame. They make large rectangular-shaped diggings as they search for food, especially in medium-sized trunks or limbs. Smaller diameter dead limbs and trees provide homes and food for smaller woodpeckers, like the hairy and downy, as well as for flying squirrels. Much larger hollow trees and stumps pro-

vide nest sites for owls and dens for raccoons, opossums, and skunks. Finally, the climax forest has a large diversity of microhabitats. For example, adjacent spots with different slope, exposure, moisture, light, and soil conditions have different mixes of species of trees.

The full range of habitats and microhabitats on the surface in the park is best seen starting at Temple Hill Cemetery on the north side of Green River. The trail starts on gentle slopes on sandstone with open oak-hickory forest. It descends sharply past sandstone and limestone outcrops to the First Creek Lake floodplain and wooded swamp. To continue, you need a topographic map and compass to head upstream. The stream valley slowly narrows, the creek stops meandering, and you come to the most spectacular surface scenery in the park. The stream undercuts and cuts through sandstone beds, forming overhangs, cliffs, and waterfalls. On the cliffs grow hanging gardens of mosses and ferns. The enclosed valley is buffered from summer drought and winter winds, so both southern and northern species of plants occur together. By the falls are northern hemlock, yew, and yellow birch, while below a falls grow southern holly along with cucumber and umbrella magnolia.

Thousands of years ago the entire forest was virgin. Bears and cougars still lived here then, and the meadows and forest provided a livelihood for people who made clever use of their resources.

CRF photo by Charles E. Mohr

Whitetail deer are commonly seen on the open grassy areas near the visitor center and along roadsides. They also thrive in successional forests recovering from the farming that was common in pre-park days. Less often seen, pack rats build nests inside cave entrances most visitors do not visit. Compulsive collectors, they will carry off small, attractive objects, like car keys, and hide them in their nests.

PEOPLE AT MAMMOTH CAVE

Humans first entered Mammoth Cave about 4,000 years ago. They left vast quantities of cultural material, including some of the earliest evidence of organized agriculture in the eastern United States. The artifacts were preserved by the dry conditions in passages underneath the sandstone caprock. Both dryness and sulfate salts prevented bacterial decay, so there is a good record of the Indians' clothing, implements, and food items from 2500 B.C. to 0 B.C.

Most of the dietary record comes from dried feces scattered throughout the cave. During the period of prehistoric cave exploration the Indians made one of the most revolutionary transitions in the history of human life—the shift from a hunting and gathering existence to cultivation of plants. At first the Indians gathered seeds of wild sunflower (*Helianthus annuus*), goosefoot or lamb's quarters (*Chenopodium* species), and sumpweed or marsh elder (*Iva annua*), a relative of the sunflower. These seeds were small—the same size as the seeds of these wild species today. Preserved seeds found with later Indian material got larger and larger over hundreds of years, showing that the people selected the largest ones each year; thus they were deliberately breeding to improve the plants.

The Indians lived seasonally in the cave entrances, eating a variety of wild plants, especially hickory nuts that could be stored. They supplemented these plant foods with occasional deer, turkey, raccoon, and other small mammals, as well as mussels and fish. In spring they ate plants like sweet flag and lily, whose roots and bulbs are high in Vitamin C, and flowers like the native dandelion, whose abundant pollen provides protein. In summer they ate wild strawberries, blackberries and raspberries; and in fall they gathered acorns.

Some of the bones found at their camps were human. They were broken, split, and marked in the same way as deer bones. Archeologists have found parts of the skeletons of at least forty-one individuals at the Salts Cave camp site, and their ages ranged from fetus to adult of both males and

females. The Indians may have practiced opportunistic or ritualistic cannibalism of enemies or of naturally deceased individuals.

The kinds of clothing and implements found show that the Indians were skilled and culturally advanced. They had not only learned to grow and improve various plants, but they also knew how to weave. Some of their fabrics were the simple over/ under weave, but often they wove a more complex chevron pattern. Leaves of canary grass and rattlesnake master along with the stringy inner bark of grapevines, pawpaw, leatherwood shrubs, and linden trees provided the fibers from which they wove slippers, breechcloths, and net bags and braided and twisted cords and ties. A few woven baskets and carved wooden bowls date from the earlier cave occupation periods, but the most recent and numerous containers were made from gourds and squash, presumably cultivated after being introduced from Middle America. They also used rock pestles for pounding, celts for carving or chopping, awls for sewing or weaving, and mussel shells as spoons or scoops. The most intriguing remains found in the cave are thousands of pieces of charred cane torches scattered throughout the cave.

Many generations of these people repeatedly entered the caves in the area and removed tons of gypsum, flint for projectile points or trading, and probably some epsomite, mirabilite, and aragonite minerals. Soot from their torches stained the walls and ceilings everywhere near the entrances of Mammoth Cave and Salts Cave (in Flint Ridge) and has been found in small crawlways as far as two and a half miles into the caves.

Their mining techniques for sulfate minerals were simple. They pounded and broke the harder gypsum crusts with rocks and scraped off the softer salts with mussel shells. They used woven fiber bags to carry the crystals and hides or bowls of gourd or wood to carry the powdered minerals back to camp.

We can only speculate about the reasons these ancient miners sought minerals. Gypsum has no

Drawing by Tomas Dougi ©Interpretive Publications, Inc.

Prehistoric people first entered Mammoth Cave some 4,000 years ago, and they used the cave for some 2,000 years. They lived in the entrances; and, using cane torches to light their way, they went deep into the cave to gather gypsum.

known medicinal value. It is soft and deteriorates quickly with weathering, and the mining sites rarely had the pretty flowers and crystals that might be used for decoration or trade. Aragonite, however, might have been sought for decoration or trade, because this crystalline form of calcium carbonate is much more spectacular and durable than gypsum. Although post-Columbian Indians used gypsum as a white pigment for paint or as plaster, "medicine," chalk, or a bleaching agent, no evidence has been found for such uses by pre-Columbian Indians of the Mammoth Cave region.

Mirabilite and epsomite salts do have medicinal properties. They are laxatives. But the Indians' high-fiber diet would make laxatives unnecessary. This does not preclude use of the sulfates in some sort of religious ceremony. Another possible use for mirabilite was as a salty seasoning.

Whatever the intended uses, the quest for cave minerals could be risky, as was vividly revealed when a desiccated body was found pinned beneath a huge slab of limestone. Apparently, while the miner was working or crawling under the slab, it slumped onto him. His body lay entombed for more than two thousand years until two guides found it in 1935. The body was so well preserved —including hair, skin, and intestinal organs—that

scientists could tell much about him. He was about forty-five years old and only five feet three inches tall. He had sound teeth and bones and only a few intestinal parasites. He was barefoot and was wearing a kind of wraparound skirt of woven fabric. Next to him were some torch fragments and a woven bag, presumably brought to carry nuts, as food, into the cave and mined crystals back to camp.

These Indians departed the Mammoth Cave area about the time of the birth of Christ, and the caves remained undisturbed for the next eighteen centuries.

CIVILIZATION COMES TO THE FRONTIER
Before 1750 few white men had seen the area that is now Kentucky. First came hunters, explorers, surveyors, and veterans of the French and Indian War. Land companies were granted huge blocks of land, and they enticed settlers with stories of endless virgin forests and prairies covered with lush grasses. By 1775 settlement had begun in earnest.

No one knows for sure the exact date Mammoth Cave was rediscovered. The legend is that a hunter named Houchin found the entrance while pursuing a bear about 1797. The first official record referring to the cave is found in the Warren

31

County Survey Book dated August 18, 1798: "Valentine Simon enters 200 acres of second rate land...lying on Green River beginning on a sycamore tree on the bank of said river thence running southward including two petre caves...." The two caves referred to were Mammoth and Dixon.

Frontiersmen had been preserving meat and making gunpowder from saltpetre for personal use and for sale for years, and Kentucky was one source of cave nitrate for the production of gunpowder during the war of 1812. In fact, Hyman Gratz and Charles Wilkins, who by 1812 owned Mammoth Cave, were professional saltpetre dealers; and they established a saltpetre leaching factory at the cave.

To prepare for the leaching operation, square wooden vats were built, and wooden pipes were made from long, straight tulip poplar logs. The logs were bored by hand-turned augers and were joined together by tapering and reaming adjacent pipes and fitting one end into another.

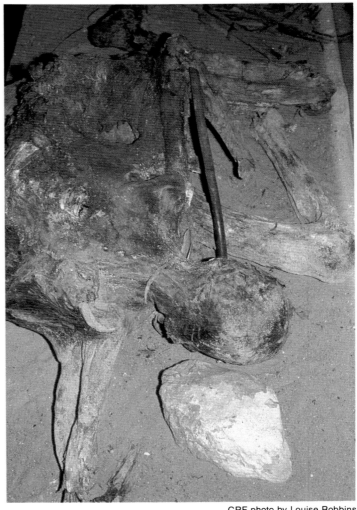

CRF photo by Louise Robbins

One of the prehistoric miners met a tragic end when a huge slab of limestone—like Giant's Coffin—slid onto him while he was working and pinned him beneath it. Some two thousand years later—in 1935—guides Grover Campbell and Lyman Cutliff discovered his body, so well preserved by the dry cave that scientists could tell his age and physical condition.

Giant's Coffin

During the War of 1812 Mammoth Cave provided saltpetre for the production of gunpowder. Slaves loaded soil into wooden vats *(above)* and saturated it with water flowing into the cave through pipes made of tulip poplar logs *(below)*. The nitrate solution that leached out of the soil was pumped to the surface through the pipes, where it underwent further processing.

Black slaves dug the cave soil, placed it into the vats, and saturated it with water flowing into the cave through the wooden pipes. The water trickled through the soil, and calcium nitrate leached out. Wooden pumps pumped the nitrate solution via the pipeline to the surface, where it was heated and poured into hoppers filled with hickory and oak wood ash. As the solution seeped through the high-potassium ash, the calcium nitrate changed to potassium nitrate (saltpetre), and the calcium precipitated as "curds" of calcium hydroxide. This mixture was filtered, then boiled to concentrate the saltpetre. When the concentrate was filtered and cooled, it crystallized. It was bagged and transported to powdermills in Philadelphia, where it was combined with powdered charcoal and sulfur to make gunpowder.

The saltpetre business was quite profitable for the owners, netting a profit of about 21 cents per pound. After the war ended, though, demand dropped, and nitrates were obtained elsewhere at a cheaper price.

MAMMOTH CAVE'S FAME GROWS

A new era for Mammoth Cave began in 1816 when it became a major visitor attraction as a result of increased publicity. Much was being written about skeletal remains found in Mammoth Cave and a prehistoric "mummy" discovered by saltpetre miners in a nearby cave.

In 1838 a new owner, Franklin Gorin, purchased Mammoth Cave; and under his guidance a new period of prosperity began. Gorin initiated a regular guide force when he brought his seventeen-year-old black slave, Stephen Bishop, to the cave. Before his death at age thirty-six, Bishop had achieved worldwide fame for his discoveries and knowledge of the cave, as well as for his wit and charm. Gorin later added two brothers, Matt and Nick Bransford, to his guide staff. They, too, were slaves, and they spent the rest of their lives at Mammoth Cave. With these men began a tradition for three and four generations of a family to work at the cave. The workers felt a strong sense of duty and pride in carrying on the legacy of their forebears, and the tradition endures even today.

Still within the 1830s the discovery of blindfish in the Echo River drew scientific attention to the cave. In 1839 the cave was sold again.

The new owner, Dr. John Croghan, had money and was a skilled promoter with great plans for developing his property. He built roads, improved buildings, and constructed a large hotel whose imposing presence dominated the shaded lawns until it burned in 1916.

Mammoth Cave continued to make the news when Dr. Croghan established the world's first (and last) underground tuberculosis hospital. He believed that the stable temperature and humidity and apparent dryness in the cave would have a curative effect on patients suffering from tuberculosis, a primary killer of that day.

Volunteer patients lived in the cave in small stone structures with canvas roofs. Their attempt to survive was pitiful. They tried to grow flowers to

The Rotunda once rang with the sounds of shovels and men's voices as slaves worked by the dim light of oil lamps to leach nitrate from the cave soil. Three large passages intersect to form this huge chamber—Houchins Narrows, Broadway, and Audubon Avenue.

Soon after Dr. John Croghan bought Mammoth Cave in 1839, he established a tuberculosis hospital in the cave. Patients lived in little stone huts with canvas roofs, but the experiment failed after only a few months when patients either died or moved out.

In those days guides encouraged visitors to the cave to erect stone monuments in Gothic Avenue dedicated to their states or clubs or themselves—a clever way to clear the rocky trails. They also wrote on the ceiling with candle smoke. The National Park Service discourages such embellishments nowadays.

add a spot of cheer to their dark surroundings; but the flowers failed to respond, just as the patients failed to respond to the treatment. After only a few months some of the invalids died, and the others left the cave. Ironically, Dr. Croghan died six years after the experiment ended—a victim of tuberculosis.

By the time Dr. Croghan died, the cave was beginning to attract many well known people. Among them were the renowned Swedish singer, Jenny Lind; Prince Alexis of Russia; Emperor of Brazil Dom Pedro; Norwegian violinist Ole Bull; lawyer/politician William Jennings Bryan; and the famous Shakespearean actor Edwin Booth. (Booth's brother, John Wilkes Booth, assassinated Abraham Lincoln.) In those days Mammoth Cave was the "in" place to go.

National Park Service

Dr. Croghan also built a large hotel to accommodate increasing numbers of visitors to the cave, who usually arrived by stagecoach. The hotel burned in 1916.

TRANSPORTATION TO MAMMOTH CAVE
Traveling in Kentucky in the early 1800s was not easy, and Mammoth Cave was not easy to reach. Rutted and rocky roads meandered here and there, following contours of hills and valleys. Dry and dusty in summer, these roads became quagmires during rainy weather.

Even though Mammoth Cave was relatively isolated, it had one advantage: proximity to the main road between Louisville, Kentucky, and Nashville, Tennessee. Stagecoaches ran intermittent-

ly during the early 1800s between those cities, and by 1816 regular runs had been established. Connections between the highway and Mammoth Cave could be made at Bell's Tavern.

Bell's Tavern lay halfway between Louisville and Nashville at Glasgow Junction (renamed Park City in 1938) and was a major waystation for the stagecoaches that traveled the route. Travelers bound for Mammoth Cave boarded a local stagecoach there for the 8.7-mile ride. Later, as trains replaced stagelines between Louisville and Nashville, visitors still rode stages from Glasgow Junction and Cave City to the cave. The arrival of a stagecoach at the Mammoth Cave Hotel was heralded by a bugle and much activity as porters set about the task of assisting the travelers.

Stagecoach travel was not without danger. One evening in 1880 a group of visitors was returning to Cave City when two horsemen suddenly appeared and stopped the stagecoach near the Little Hope Cemetery. The bandits took more than $1,000 in cash and personal property from the passengers. One item, taken from Judge R. H. Rountree of Lebanon, Kentucky, was a fine gold watch engraved with his name. Later, a newspaper story reported that the watch was found on Jesse James when he was killed in Missouri—evidence that Jesse James had robbed the Mammoth Cave stagecoach.

Transportation greatly improved in 1886 with

the establishment of the Mammoth Cave Railroad, which connected Mammoth Cave with the L & N line at Glasgow Junction. Not only did this line help travelers, but it also provided easy access to town for local people. It was not uncommon for the train crew to run shopping errands for housewives and deliver the items on the return trip. Local youths sometimes hitched rides on the train. More often than not the conductor would discover them and put them off, but that was no problem; it was part of the game. They repaid the conductor's diligence by soaping the rails on his return trip, which caused the train to stall.

Pulled by the engine Hercules, the little train served Mammoth Cave for forty-three years until 1929, when the increasing use of automobiles replaced it. All that remains today of this spur line is one span of tracks, the engine Hercules, and one coach—artifacts of a passing era of transportation.

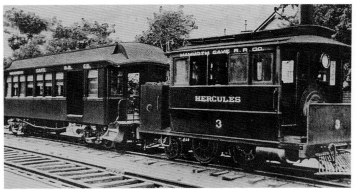

For forty-three years the Mammoth Cave Railroad carried travelers from Glasgow Junction (now named Park City) to the cave. Only the engine Hercules and a short span of tracks near the visitor center now remain.

Until electric lights were installed, visitors toured the cave's wonders by lantern light, and guides illuminated the darkest recesses of large chambers by throwing torches into them. Nowadays, a lantern tour is available to simulate that experience, and guides on the Historic Tour treat visitors to a demonstration of torch throwing in Methodist Church. This room is so named because church services and weddings used to be conducted here.

EXPLORATION

The most dramatic chapter in man's association with Mammoth Cave deals with exploration. The pre-Columbian Indians who first entered the caves in the area about 2000 B.C. were the first explorers. We still do not know whether they were only searching for minerals or were also driven by a spirit of adventure. With only torches to light their way, these people thoroughly traversed complex passageways as much as two and a half miles from any present entrance.

In 1964 six researchers from the Cave Research Foundation reconstructed the way caving by torchlight was probably done. In bare feet, wearing only shorts to simulate Indian clothing, and carrying torches of the same species of cane and weed stalks that had been found in the cave, they spent five hours walking and crawling underground. After some experimentation, they found that a torch of four or five canes about three feet long

worked well. The warm orange light from the torches provided better illumination than modern carbide lamps. On the average, such a torch lasted nearly an hour. Moreover, in spite of the chilly temperature in the cave and their scanty dress, they did not feel uncomfortable. Thus, they dramatically demonstrated that, with ample supplies of torch materials, a party of Indians could easily have spent a dozen hours or more comfortably working and exploring underground.

Beginning in 1838, Stephen Bishop made many excursions into unknown areas of the cave. Imagine you are standing at the brink of a yawning hole deep within the dark cave. The flickering light from your lantern dances on the fluted walls but does not reach the bottom of the abyss. You and your companion have brought a ladder, which the two of you now place across the chasm. Your friend holds the lantern high while you ease yourself onto the ladder and inch your way across

Cave passages lie under four ridges of the Mammoth Cave Plateau—Joppa Ridge, Mammoth Cave Ridge, Toohey Ridge, and Flint Ridge. As of the end of 1984 about 300 miles had been surveyed by Cave Research Foundation and Central Kentucky Karst Coalition teams. The arrow marks the Historic Entrance. Great Onyx Cave, shown on this map, is not part of Mammoth Cave, although a passage in Mammoth runs beneath it.

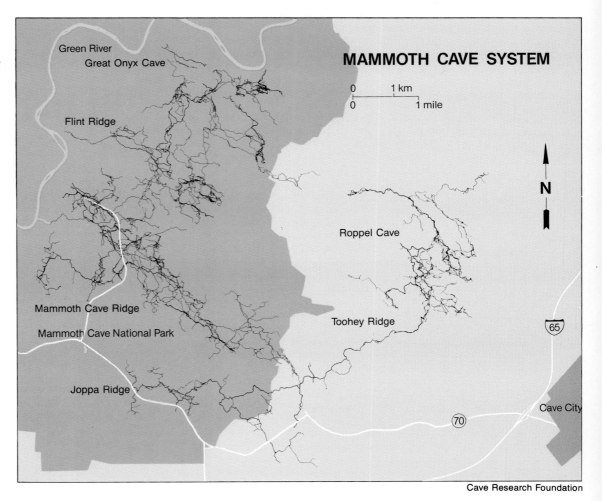

MAMMOTH CAVE SYSTEM

Cave Research Foundation

CRF photo by Pete Lindsley

For decades Mammoth Cave has lured adventurers and scientists. To connect the cave passages in the different ridges to each other, explorers must work their way under the valleys separating the ridges, where the passages become very small and sometimes very wet. (Here, CRF explorers examine a river bank.) Although the cave severely tests their strength, endurance, and skill, these daring men and women return again and again to explore and study the cave's vast labyrinth. Their discoveries continue to disclose the cave's secrets.

it, not daring to look down. Finally, with great relief, you reach the other side. This is how Bishop must have first crossed Bottomless Pit. He explored the passageways beyond as well and discovered Echo River and many other sites included on public tours today.

In the early 1920's, Edmund Turner and Floyd Collins, developers of the Great Onyx and Crystal caves in Flint Ridge, explored those caves and discovered many new passages. At about the same time, George Morrison discovered the New Entrance to Mammoth Cave. Although a well seasoned caver, Floyd Collins became trapped in nearby Sand Cave in 1925. An intensive, highly publicized rescue effort was mounted, but rescuers were unable to extricate him before he died.

In the 1930s, Claude and Leo Hunt and Carl and Pete Hanson worked as guides at Mammoth Cave and explored new sections of the cave. They found the New Discovery section of Mammoth Cave in 1938.

Beginning in 1947, sustained exploration in the area focused mainly on Flint Ridge. The managers of Mammoth Onyx Cave and Floyd Collins' Crystal Cave encouraged exploration and research in the Flint Ridge caves.

In 1954, the National Speleological Society sponsored a week-long expedition to survey more than two miles of passages in Flint Ridge. The expedition was noteworthy for developing a more scientific approach to cave exploration.

In 1957, some members of that expedition incorporated the Cave Research Foundation to support exploration, research, interpretation, and conservation of caves. Its volunteer cavers began by intensively exploring, surveying, mapping, and studying the caves. They discovered a vast, undisturbed network of passages in Flint Ridge and dreamed like others before them of finding a connection between Flint Ridge and Mammoth Cave Ridge. That connection would necessarily be deep, for it would have to pass beneath the valley separating the two ridges.

Finally, the dream of a hundred years became reality. On September 9, 1972, a group departed from a point on Flint Ridge. After a grueling twelve-hour, six-mile trip squeezing through tiny passages under Houchins Valley; walking, crawling, and wriggling on bellies through dust, mud, and water; and finally wading in neck-deep water with less than a foot of airspace below the ceiling, five men and one woman emerged into the Echo River in Cascade Hall in Mammoth Cave. Patricia

41

Crowther, John Wilcox, Richard Zopf, Steve Wells, and Gary Eller of the Cave Research Foundation and Cleve Pinnix of the National Park Service had finally discovered the Big Connection. This discovery made the Mammoth Cave System unquestionably the longest in the world. (The second longest cave system is Optimisticeskaja in the USSR; the third longest is Hölloch Höhle in Switzerland.) Instead of returning the way they had come, the explorers walked to the Snowball Dining Room and left by way of the elevator!

Even though the dream of the Big Connection had been realized, exploration continued. In 1979 the smaller Joppa Ridge system was connected to

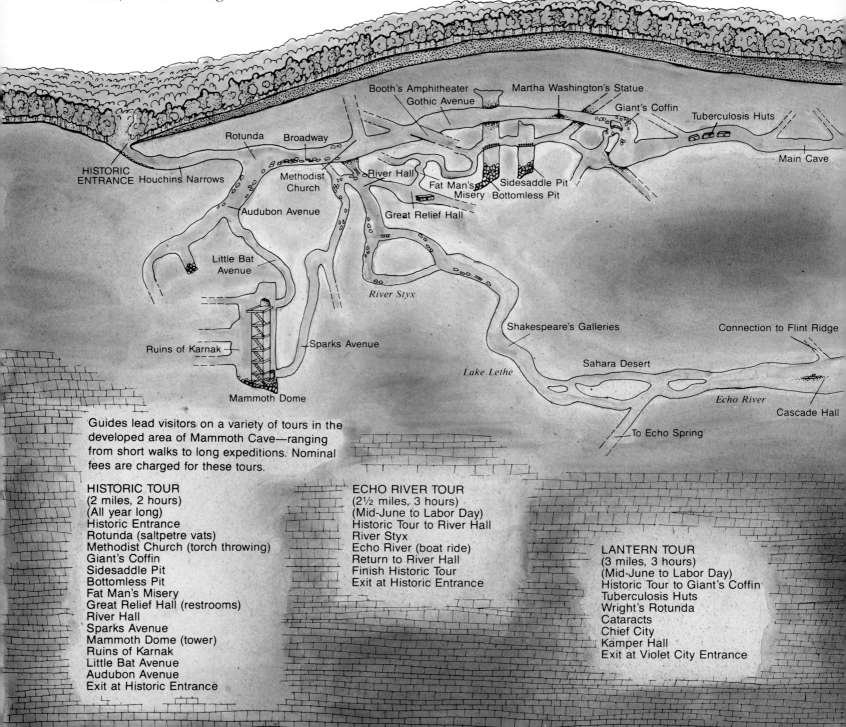

Guides lead visitors on a variety of tours in the developed area of Mammoth Cave—ranging from short walks to long expeditions. Nominal fees are charged for these tours.

HISTORIC TOUR
(2 miles, 2 hours)
(All year long)
Historic Entrance
Rotunda (saltpetre vats)
Methodist Church (torch throwing)
Giant's Coffin
Sidesaddle Pit
Bottomless Pit
Fat Man's Misery
Great Relief Hall (restrooms)
River Hall
Sparks Avenue
Mammoth Dome (tower)
Ruins of Karnak
Little Bat Avenue
Audubon Avenue
Exit at Historic Entrance

ECHO RIVER TOUR
(2½ miles, 3 hours)
(Mid-June to Labor Day)
Historic Tour to River Hall
River Styx
Echo River (boat ride)
Return to River Hall
Finish Historic Tour
Exit at Historic Entrance

LANTERN TOUR
(3 miles, 3 hours)
(Mid-June to Labor Day)
Historic Tour to Giant's Coffin
Tuberculosis Huts
Wright's Rotunda
Cataracts
Chief City
Kämper Hall
Exit at Violet City Entrance

Leo Hunt (left) and Pete Hanson (right) explored new sections of Mammoth Cave while working at the cave as guides during the 1930s. When explorers from Flint Ridge found Pete's initials on a wall deep in the cave, they knew they had found their way into Mammoth Cave—but they did not know *where* they were. A later expedition pressed on beyond this spot and at last emerged into Cascade Hall, finally completing the connection of the Flint Ridge and Mammoth Cave systems in 1972.

National Park Service

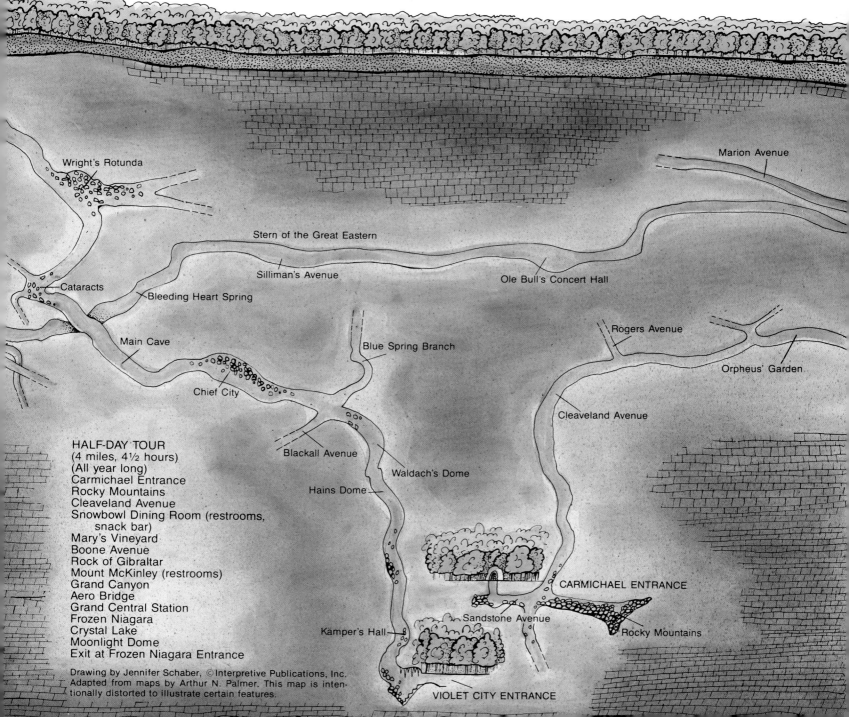

Wright's Rotunda

Marion Avenue

Stern of the Great Eastern

Silliman's Avenue

Ole Bull's Concert Hall

Cataracts

Bleeding Heart Spring

Main Cave

Blue Spring Branch

Rogers Avenue

Orpheus' Garden

Chief City

Cleaveland Avenue

Blackall Avenue

HALF-DAY TOUR
(4 miles, 4½ hours)
(All year long)
Carmichael Entrance
Rocky Mountains
Cleaveland Avenue
Snowbowl Dining Room (restrooms, snack bar)
Mary's Vineyard
Boone Avenue
Rock of Gibraltar
Mount McKinley (restrooms)
Grand Canyon
Aero Bridge
Grand Central Station
Frozen Niagara
Crystal Lake
Moonlight Dome
Exit at Frozen Niagara Entrance

Waldach's Dome

Hains Dome

CARMICHAEL ENTRANCE

Sandstone Avenue

Rocky Mountains

Kämper's Hall

VIOLET CITY ENTRANCE

Drawing by Jennifer Schaber, ©Interpretive Publications, Inc. Adapted from maps by Arthur N. Palmer. This map is intentionally distorted to illustrate certain features.

Mammoth Cave, and in 1983 Roppel Cave was connected to the growing system.

Exploration, mapping, and research have been able to progress hand-in-hand at Mammoth Cave largely because the National Park Service provides continuity by giving protection, support, and encouragement. Increasingly accurate and sophisti-cated computer-drawn maps provide baselines for better biological, archeological, geological, and hydrological studies. Some of these studies in turn suggest where new passages should be found. On the basis of this evidence, there is the potential for at least five hundred miles of passages to be discovered! Mammoth Cave will continue to attract explorers and scientists as well as tourists because of its truly unique combination of features.

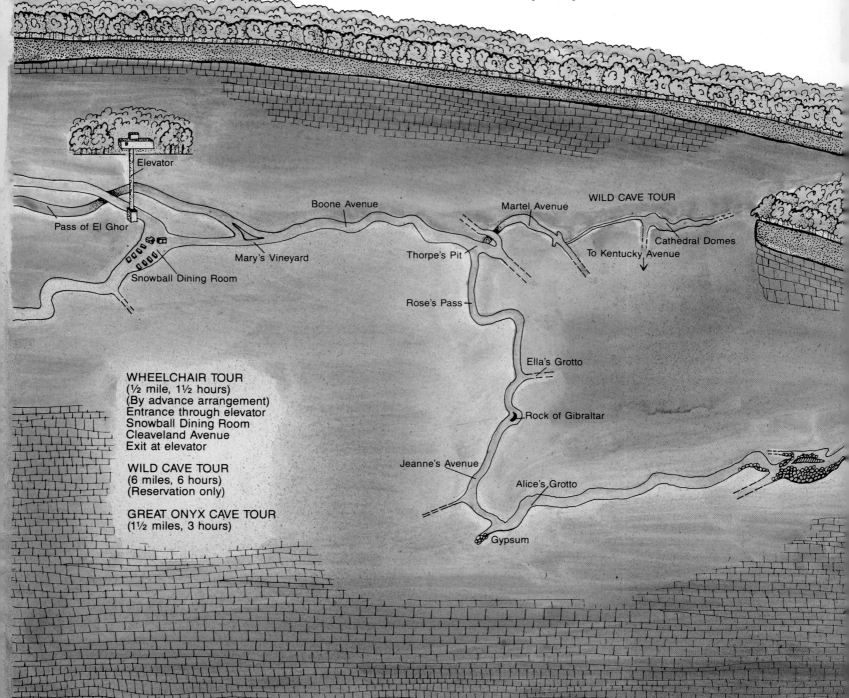

Elevator

Pass of El Ghor

Boone Avenue

Martel Avenue

WILD CAVE TOUR

Mary's Vineyard

Thorpe's Pit

Cathedral Domes

To Kentucky Avenue

Snowball Dining Room

Rose's Pass

Ella's Grotto

WHEELCHAIR TOUR
(½ mile, 1½ hours)
(By advance arrangement)
Entrance through elevator
Snowball Dining Room
Cleaveland Avenue
Exit at elevator

Rock of Gibraltar

WILD CAVE TOUR
(6 miles, 6 hours)
(Reservation only)

Jeanne's Avenue

Alice's Grotto

GREAT ONYX CAVE TOUR
(1½ miles, 3 hours)

Gypsum

For an unusual adventure, the Wild Cave Tour offers visitors a taste of cave exploring. The rigorous tour lasts six hours. It is available on a reservation-only basis during the summer.

FROZEN NIAGARA TOUR
(1½ miles, 1½ hours)
(All year long)
Frozen Niagara Entrance
Onyx Chamber
Crystal Lake
Moonlight Dome
Frozen Niagara
Flat Ceiling
Exit at Frozen Niagara Entrance

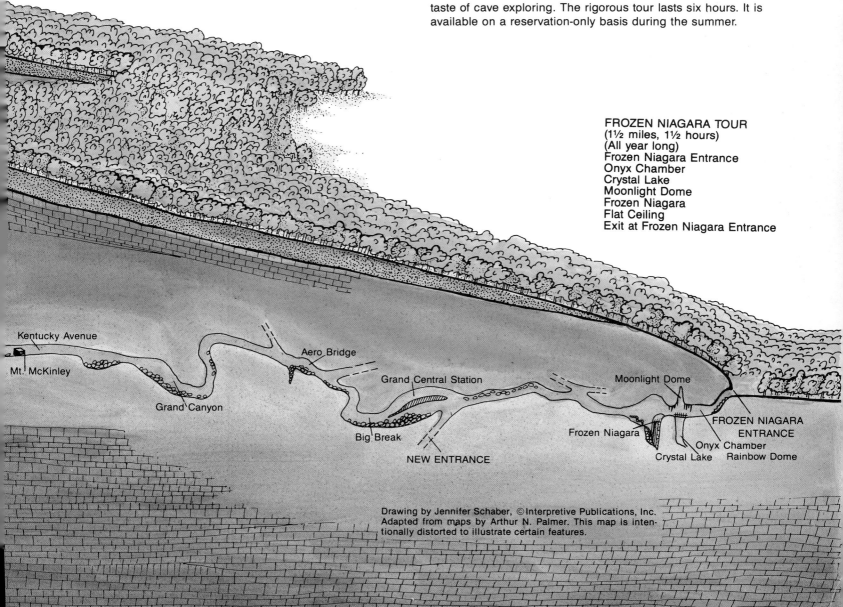

Kentucky Avenue

Mt. McKinley

Grand Canyon

Aero Bridge

Grand Central Station

Big Break

NEW ENTRANCE

Moonlight Dome

Frozen Niagara

Crystal Lake

FROZEN NIAGARA ENTRANCE

Onyx Chamber

Rainbow Dome

Drawing by Jennifer Schaber, ©Interpretive Publications, Inc.
Adapted from maps by Arthur N. Palmer. This map is intentionally distorted to illustrate certain features.

MAMMOTH CAVE NATIONAL PARK

On July 1, 1941, Mammoth Cave officially became the twenty-sixth national park to enter the National Park System. The park's 52,370 acres offer many opportunities for recreation.

National Park Service guides lead walks over shaded trails to such interesting places as Green River Bluffs and River Styx Spring, where water exits the cave. Interpreters present folkway or campfire programs. The Nolin and Green rivers in the park offer boating and fishing. More than thirty miles of trails invite hikers. Opportunities range from an easy walk near the visitor center to backpacking north of the Green River along trails through midsuccessional forest with rock bluffs and springs. A motor nature trail passes through early second-growth forest that is rapidly reclaiming old homesites, as well as through a forest that has long been undisturbed.

Cave tours are available throughout the year for everyone—young and old, vigorous and disabled. They range from one-and-a-half-hour strolls to six-hour adventures. On all the tours interpreters tell the story of Mammoth Cave, as their fathers and grandfathers may have done before them.

A WORLD HERITAGE

Not only is Mammoth Cave one of the United States' premier national parks, but it is also an international treasure preserved for all peoples of the world. It was so recognized in October 1981, when the United Nations Educational, Scientific and Cultural Organization (UNESCO) voted to place Mammoth Cave National Park on its list of World Heritage Sites.

In 1972, the member nations of UNESCO adopted the "Convention for the Protection of the World Cultural and Natural Heritage" to provide the means to protect cultural and natural monuments and sites common to the heritage of all peoples of the world, now, and in the future.

With more than three hundred miles of mapped passages, the clearest and most complete record of geomorphic and climatic changes in the past 10 to 20 million years of any readily accessible continental feature anywhere, the most diverse cave ecosystem in the world, the greatest variety of sulfate minerals of any cave anywhere, and unequaled information on one of the earliest horticultural societies in North America, the world's longest cave is undoubtedly one of the earth's most astounding masterworks and one of man's most renowned treasures. Its story reminds us of the ingenuity, courage, and folly of men—and the eternal power, complexity, and glory of nature.

ADDITIONAL READING

Brucker, Roger W., and Richard A. Watson. *The Longest Cave* (New York: Alfred A. Knopf, 1976).

Bullitt, Alexander Clark. *Rambles in Mammoth Cave* (St. Louis: Cave Books, 1985).

Crowther, Patricia P. et al. *The Grand Kentucky Junction* (St. Louis: Cave Books, 1984).

Culver, David C. *Cave Life: Evolution and Ecology* (Cambridge: Harvard University Press, 1982).

Faller, Adolph. The Plant Ecology of Mammoth Cave National Park Kentucky. (Ph.D. dissertation, Indiana State University, Terre Haute, 1975. Number 75-29871 Xerox University Microfilms, Ann Arbor, MI 48106.)

Finkel, Donald. *Going Under* (New York: Atheneum, 1978).

Jackson, Donald D. *Underground Worlds* (Arlington, Va.: Time-Life Books).

Lawrence, Joe Jr., and Roger W. Brucker. *The Caves Beyond* (Teaneck, N.J.: Zephyrus Press, 1975).

Meloy, Harold. *Mummies of Mammoth Cave* (Shelbyville, Ind.: Micron, 1971).

Mohr, Charles E., and Thomas L. Poulson. *The Life of the Cave*, Our Living World of Nature Series (New York: McGraw-Hill, 1966).

Moore, George W., and G. Nicholas Sullivan. *Speleology: The Study of Caves* (St. Louis: Cave Books, 1981).

Murray, Robert A., and Roger W. Brucker. *Trapped!* (Lexington, Ky.: University Press of Kentucky, 1979).

Palmer, Arthur N. *A Geological Guide to Mammoth Cave National Park* (Teaneck, N.J.: Zephyrus Press, 1981).

Watson, Patty Jo, editor, *Archeology of the Mammoth Cave Area* (New York: Academic Press, 1974).

(Inside back cover): Mammoth Cave's underground rivers eventually emerge as springs, like River Styx Spring, and empty into the Green River.